My Creators

Dedicated to

Maxine and Harry Rose

and

Anyone who reads this and has never

had a book dedicated to them.

This has been the hardest story I've ever written. My memories are filled with many choices. Who should I chose? What events should I select? I've been lucky. Most of my life has surrounded me with good people who've given me: laughter, happiness, stories to tell, forgiveness for my failures, love, and then gave me Jackie who filled it all with life.

No one I've known has had more fun living than I've had.

Heaven can't beat it.

Could it be that this is heaven for some, hell for the rest?

—George Spain

MY CREATORS

George Spain

Ideas into Books: Westview®
Kingston Springs, Tennessee

***Ideas into Books*®**
W E S T V I E W
P.O. Box 605
Kingston Springs, TN 37082
www.publishedbywestview.com

ISBN 978-1-62880-219-1

First edition, March 2021

Printed in the United States of America on acid free paper.

"For dust you are and to dust you will return."

Genesis 3:19

Between these dusts I've had many creators.
This is my appreciation to them.

THE FIRST BOOK OF MOSES, CALLED

GENESIS.

CHAP. I.

1 *The creation of heaven and earth, 3 of the light,*
6 of the firmament, 9 of the earth separated from
the waters, 11 and made fruitful, 14 of the sun,
moon, and stars, 20 of fish and fowl, 24 of beasts
and cattle, 26 of man in the image of God. 29
Also the appointment of food.

IN the ᵃbeginning ᵇGod created the heaven and the earth.

2 And the earth was without form, and void; and darkness *was* upon the face of the deep: ᶜand the Spirit of God moved upon the face of the waters.

3 ᵈAnd God said, ᵉLet there be light: and there was light.

4 And God saw the light, that *it was* good: and God divided †the light from the darkness.

5 And God called the light ᶠDay, and the darkness he called Night: †and the evening and the morning were the first day.

6 ¶ And God said, ᵍLet there be a †firmament in the midst of the waters: and let it divide the waters from the waters.

7 And God made the firmament, ʰand divided the waters which *were* under the firmament from the waters which *were* ⁱabove the firmament: and it was so.

8 And God called the firmament Heaven: and the evening and the morning were the second day.

9 ¶ And God said, ᵏLet the waters under the heaven be gathered together unto one place, and let the dry *land* appear: and it was so.

10 And God called the dry *land* Earth; and the gathering together of the waters called he Seas: and God saw that *it was* good.

11 And God said, Let the earth ˡbring forth †grass, the herb yielding seed, *and* the fruit-tree yielding ᵐfruit after his kind, whose seed *is* in itself, upon the earth: and it was so.

12 And the earth brought forth grass, *and* herb yielding seed after his kind, and the tree yielding fruit, whose seed *was* in itself, after his kind: and God saw that *it was* good.

13 And the evening and the morning were the third day.

14 ¶ And God said, Let there be ⁿlights in the firmament of the heaven, to divide †the day from the night: and let them be for signs, and ᵒfor seasons, and for days, and years.

15 And let them be for lights in the firmament of the heaven to give light upon the earth: and it was so.

16 And God ᵖmade two great lights; the greater light †to rule the day, and ᑫthe lesser light to rule the night: *he made* ʳthe stars also.

17 And God set them in the firmament of the heaven to give light upon the earth,

18 And to ˢrule over the day, and over the night, and to divide the light from the darkness: and God saw that *it was* good.

19 And the evening and the morning were the fourth day.

20 And God said, Let the waters bring forth abundantly the ‖moving creature that hath †life, and †fowl *that* may fly above the earth in the †open firmament of heaven.

21 And ᵗGod created great whales, and every living creature that moveth, which the waters brought forth abundantly after their kind, and every winged fowl after his kind: and God saw that *it was* good.

22 And God blessed them, saying, ᵘBe fruitful, and multiply, and fill the waters in the seas, and let fowl multiply in the earth.

23 And the evening and the morning were the fifth day.

24 ¶ And God said, Let the earth bring forth the living creature after his kind, cattle, and creeping thing, and beast of the earth after his kind: and it was so.

25 And God made the beast of the earth after his kind, and cattle after their kind, and every thing that creepeth upon the earth after his kind: and God saw that *it was* good.

26 ¶ And God said, ˣLet us make man in our image, after our likeness: and ʸlet them have dominion over the fish of the sea, and over the fowl of the air, and over the cattle, and over all the earth, and over every creeping thing that creepeth upon the earth.

3

From the Darwin, Lynch, Spain Family Bible

Genesis 1

"In the beginning God created the heavens and the earth." And in verse 27, "So God created man in his own image, in the image of God, he created him, male and female he created them." Genesis 1: 1 and 27

And then along came Charles Darwin and the Origin of Species, "It is interesting to contemplate a tangled bank, clothed with many plants of many kinds, with birds singing on the bushes, with various insects flitting about, and with worms crawling through the damp earth, and to reflect that these elaborately constructed forma, so different from each other, and dependent upon each other in so complex a manner; have all been produced by laws acting around us, which we are capable of conceiving, namely the production of higher animals...There is a grandeur of this view of life, with its several powers, having been originally breathed by the Creator into a few forms or into one; and that, whilst this planet has gone cycling on according to the fixed laws of gravity, from so simple a beginning, endless forms most beautiful and most wonderful have been, and are being evolved."

And then came Sigmund Freud, " "There is a powerful force within us, an unilluminated part of the mind – separated from the conscious mind that is constantly at work molding our thought, feelings, and actions.

But more than God, or Darwin, or Freud there are: many that touched my life me and played a big part in creating me. They tend to shake their heads, curse, or turn their heads away if you ask them if that's so.

The author, George Spain, at Buggytop Cave, Franklin County, Tennessee.

I am a southerner born in Nashville, Tennessee. I live only a few miles from my childhood home. Jackie, my wife was born in Memphis; her voice was "Old South." Our five children were born in Nashville. We are "Southerners." Thank the Good Lord.

Jackie Burton Spain at Lost Cove.

Next two pages: The author and Jackie's family at Big South Fork, where they went for fifteen years to ride horseback. Adam (far right on top row) was killed on his second tour to Afghanistan in 2010. Back row, left to right: Lori, Lynch, Sara, Brad, Trina, Angie, Adam. Front row: Creed, Pearson, Izzy, Jesse, Lillie, Lealand, Anna, Leah, Shane, a friend, Jackie, and George.

Rit holding the author.

When I was born former slaves and slave owners and Civil War soldiers were still alive. Now, eighty-four years later, in 2020, the world has been smote by a virus called Covid-19. Nearing the end of the year a million and quarter people have died in the world, 250,000 of these are Americans, and the numbers continue to leap higher and higher day after day.

In between these periods, great events occurred: WW11, wars in Vietnam, Iraq, Afghanistan, interplanetary rockets, the moon walk, polio vaccine developed as science and research leapt forward improving our lives, television expanded our knowledge and entertainment, and on and on- so many I can't remember nor have ever known.

This story is about my wondering who we humans are, why are we here, how did we come to be, who or what created us, maybe even, where are we going? More and more these and other questions arise in me.

I'll begin with my grandparents – outwardly so different, both sets had profound and wonderful influences on creating my views of life – especially of people – they are in me still, appearing in my books over and over, so different, but yet, both so loving.

The Spains

Now, as to the Spain's – there were lots of them: hill and hollow people, rich with intelligence and laughter; a few made whiskey and a few of those went to prison. George Stainback Spain,"Papa", my grandfather, was a foxhunting tinsmith who on occasion made beautiful, copper stills. He looked like an Indian: olive skin, facial structure, black hair. Four grandfathers back of him was James Vann; half-Scot, half Cherokee, a great but violent leader. It is said that the following was written on a board over his grave –

> "Here lies the body of James Vann.
> He killed many a white man.
> At last by rifle ball he fell,
> And devils dragged him off to hell."

Chief James Vann

And here's how his blood flowed into the Spain's –

John Vann (1747-1829) - Wah-li)

*****Chief James Vann (1768-1809)** - Jeanie-Foster

Sally Vann (1794-?) – Evan Nicholson

Mary Nicholson 91834-1892) – James Peebles

Bell Peebles (1855-1891) – Robert Spain

George Stainback Spain (1883-1965) – Clevia Frazer

George Joseph Spain (1910-1973) – Fannie Elizabeth Crossley

George Edward Spain (1936-) – Jacquelyn Katrine "Jackie" Burton

George Bradford Spain (1959-)

Thomas Lynch Spain (1960-)

Elizabeth Katrine Spain Flynn (1962-)

*****Adam Burton Spain (1966-2010)**

Matthew Darwin Spain (1969-)

*Adam was killed by a roadside bomb in Afghanistan on May 6

There is a certain comfort knowing I have James Vann' blood and genes in me, that if I do anything bad I'm not to blame – it's the Vann blood and genes that made me do it.

"Mama" Spain was a Frazer. Her father's people were Scots. One of them – allegedly a redheaded one – had passed through Columbia, Tennessee and left his seed inside her mother. Mama was illegitimate – and had red hair which she passed on to some of my female cousins. She had ten children she raised in the hills where she ruled her roost.

"Mama" and "Papa" Spain, George Stainback and Clevia Frazier Spain

Now, let's get to my father, George Joseph Spain, the oldest son. He didn't look a speck like an Indian; in fact, he looked more like a strong, well to do, gangster with his slick-oiled hair, diamond rings, gold watch, finely-tailored suits and shined shoes covering his well-fed girth. He never drank in front of us (my mother's commandment). A couple of times I took him to "dry out." He liked to gamble, loved boxing, wrestling, selling Cadillacs, living life well and, most of all he loved his family.

Elizabeth and Georgie Spain, the author's parents.

The Crossley's –

The Crossley homeplace, built by Levi Thomas Crossley in Schochoh, Kentucky.
This homeplace is still in the family.

Levi Thomas Crossley and Lillie Jane Turner Crossley were my mother's parents. Born in northern Wales "Granddaddy" ran away from home to Liverpool, England when he was nine. There he was hired on as a "cabin boy". From there he sailed on Clippers and Windjammers over the oceans of the globe for twenty years. Once, when I was four or five, I was sitting in his lap as he told me stories of his adventures on the sea. His left forearm was across my lap; on it was a faded tattoo of an anchor. As I rolled a newspaper page and made a taper for him to light his pipe from the coal fire before us, I could smell the rich smoke mixed with his King Leo peppermint candy and the plowed earth of his fields as he began to tell me of his adventures upon the sea and, as he did, I began to smell the salt air and hear the roaring of wind and waves crashing against the hull of his ship.

The Crossleys at their homeplace in Schochoh, Kentucky. Back row: L.T., Billy, and Elizateth "Fannie." Fannie was the author's mother. Front row: the author's grandparents, Levi Thomas "Granddaddy" and Lillie Jane "Grandmother," with their beautiful Collie stock dog.

Eventually, he rose to the rank of first mate. The long days and hours at sea aboard a sailing ship became his school where he came to love reading and learning from books. How fortunate I am to have the few that were not given away. As I write they are here beside me in an enclosed bookshelf.

Levi Thomas Crossley holding George Spain in his lap, and "Uncle" Jim.

Here is a story he told me as I sat on his lap. He pulled his pipe from his mouth, "Now I will tell you of a fearsome place at the end of South America called Cape Horn We were a week out of Liverpool. As we came to the Horn the wind and rain picked up and furled the sails." His voice seemed to come from far away. I looked up; his eyes were staring into the fire, "And then we were there…the great waves rolled our ship from side to side; it pitched us upward then dropped into a valley with black walls of water all around; they would have buried us if we had not been lifted up and away onto the white crest of a giant wave.

Lillie Jane Turner, "Grandmother" was a Tennessean. Her father, Jerimiah Turner, joined the Seventh Tennessee in Gallatin when it was formed in late May 1861. His regiment went to Virginia and fought in all of Lee's battles until the end. One week before Appomattox, when he was taken prisoner. He and his wife, Sarah, are buried beside one another beneath the trees of Red River Cemetery near Schochoh.

Grandmother was a teacher. Not an especially pretty woman in her old age; she had a kind face that never had make up. Her hair was always rolled up into a bun on top of her head. She was good to me and my sisters. I look back in smiles on those summer and winter weeks I spent on the Crossley farm from the time I was four of five when she tucked me under the quilts at night, checked the coal fire and heard my prayer, "Now I lay me down to sleep. I pray the Lord my soul to keep. If I die before I wake, I pray the Lord my soul to take. God bless Mama and Daddy and..." And, as I prayed, I could hear the deep sounds of bullfrogs at the pond calling and, at the end of my prayer, I'd say, "Those bullfrogs are gonna get you Grandmother and she would laugh as she kissed me with a, "Sleep tight an' don't let the bedbugs bite." She and Granddaddy are buried in Whippoorwill Cemetery in Schochoh. You can see their home a half mile away across the fields.

My father's and mother's families gave me intelligence, a love to remember their stories and laughter, and - what should I call it – the calm quietness of books that came from Granddaddy and the wildness from Papa's blood.

The author with his parents

Most of all they gave me my parents, though I should say, "our" parents to include my younger sisters, Jane and Jill. Mama and Daddy formed me and brought me into life. How fortunate I've been that it was them. They gave me intelligence, an ok body, generosity, and taught me how to love and how I should treat others and surrounded me with nice things and sent me to David Lipscomb, a private school, which I attended from the first grade through college graduation – I entered when I was four.

Left to right: The author, Jill, Jane, and Georgie

My creation began inside my mother, Fannie Elizabeth Crossley Spain. My life outside of her began on October 5, 1936 in St. Thomas Hospital. I have many black and white Brownie photos of my family when I was a little boy. On the next page is one of my mother Can you can see her through my words? July, 1937 –

Grace Crossley Shelton, Fannnie Elizabeth Crossley Spain, and Alice Johnson (friend)
Walking down Church Street, Nashville, Tennessee.

Wrapped in an expensive, full-length, mink coat, smiling to beat the band, Fannie struts her stuff between her sister Gracie, on the left, and their friend, Alice – three fine looking women parading down Church Street in Nashville. With little feather on top of her hat and a big smile, Fannie is by far the cutest of the three.

My friend, Barbara Watson, worked with her in the Children's Department at Cain Sloan Department Store. She said, "Your mother was my mentor, she helped me, she was kind and happy."

She was a good mother: hugging us, saying, "I love you", dressing and feeding us well, teaching us good manners, seeing to our attending David Lipscomb, a fine, private Christian school, loving on us when we were sick or hurting, making cakes for birthdays and parties – and Oh yes, I knew she loved me.

Now here comes "Georgie". I've already written about him in, How My Father Captured [with a little help] The Number One Car Thief And Escape Artist "Road Runner Rigsby." Here he is –

"Though my father only completed the eighth grade he, like his parents, had a first class brain and world class ambition to raise himself and his family upward, which he did by being the best new and used car dealer in Nashville. This ambition allowed me to be the first Spain to graduate from college.

"George Joseph Spain, my father, was big. He wore expensive silk suits, fine shoes, gold watches and diamond rings, his nails manicured to glistening, and his hair was oiled close to his scalp. He could have passed as a successful gangster. Known as the "Cadillac Man", he sold the finest cars at George Spain Motor Company, and those he drove glowed like the diamonds on his fingers. He liked drinking and gambling, policemen, politicians, and knew folks living on the edge, some of whom were in the numbers racket." He may have occasionally enjoyed the ladies; though I have no personal proof, I once got a hint of it from two good looking models in Cain Sloan Department Store when I worked there.

He liked to drink. I guess he was an episodic alcoholic. He'd go on binges. When that happened Mother wouldn't let him be around us so he'd go to his parents or motel until he dried out. When I was working in mental health I took him to detoxification units.

He left religion to Fannie. A few years before he died he was baptized.

He could be tough, real tough, when another man began to curse and act rude he would tell them to stop and if they didn't – as I saw once, when I was five, at a street-boxers match - he grabbed the man up by his shirt and knocked him back into his chair.

But, with all this, it was his kindness and helpfulness to his family that made him the good man that he was the father I still love.

From top: George Joseph Spain, George Stainback "Papa" Spain, George Edward Spain, George Bradford Spain

The Spain stone in Whipporwill Cemetary, Schochoh, Kentucky, Fannie and Georgie.

My sister, Jane, and I are close, we talk weekly - not so with Jill, with whom we have no communication, I do not recall, nor explain fully to myself why this is so with Jill, so I will not attempt to explain – she went her separate way.

Santa, Jill Spain, the author, Kitty Williams, and Jane Spain.

The greatest love of my life, Jacqulyn Katrine Burton, "Jackie", entered my world in early fall, 1954 just before enrollment at Lipscomb. She got out of the back of a red Lincoln in front of the girl's dorm. I was lying directly across on the steps of the boy's dorm watching the freshman girls arrive – I was a sophomore. The Lord have mercy, she was beauty and cuteness all wrapped up in one bundle.

George and Jackie

I hit the ground leaping like a deer as I ran toward her car from which a stunning woman and an ordinary looking man – her parents - were just getting out of.

All out of breath I garbled as I came up to her, "Uh...Uh...can I help take your bags in...can I help out...uh...can I help...uh...my name's George Spain."

She smiled, thanked me, and nodded to a bag, "Get that one." And on that day she became my friend, and two years later in June she married me. And we had five children, and adventures the world over and, Lord, Lord you can't imagine all that we did, and some of it I ain't gonna tell. But you can find out a lot more about her in a book Trina and I edited about her titled, "Jackie, Her Words and Words About Her."

And here's one last thing about her – she could be tough as a railroad spike which she once used on me with her fist against the side of my head because of my misbegotten ways with women. But, in time, her forgiveness and love took over again and I changed my ways. And from then on, Lord – Lord!

Next two pages: "The Herd" of friends on New Year's Eve.

First row, left to right: George "Jo Jo" Brazil, Jerry Henderson, George Spain, Jimmy "Shug" Davey.

Second Row: Nancy Jennings, Mary Brazil, Jane Myers, Trish Boone, Jackie Johnson, Evelyn Davey, Bernie Arnold, Jackie Spain.

Third Row: Jerry Jennings, Jane Davis, John Davis, Diane Olive, Terry Olive, Nick Boone, Charles Hailey, Betty Hailey, Henry "Buddy" Arnold.

Though I've had several professional opportunities to move, I've never taken them. I've never lived further than twenty miles from where I was born. Long ago I decided that the love and support from my family, close friends, and colleagues were more important than higher professional advancement and more money. Middle Tennessee beats the devil out of London and New Orleans hands down. Now, nearing the end of my life, I can say that has proven to be a great truth. Splendid are the people I love, they lift me up in all weather. Soon we'll all be gone, leaving the paths of love and care with our family and friends for our children and grandchildren to follow, if they so choose.

Captured at the historic signing of the new Title 33 Legislation.

Advocates and state officials watch as Governor Don Sundquist signs into law revisions to Title 33 of the Tennessee Code Annotated. Pictured from left to right: Andy Fox, C. Richard Treadway, M.D., Mary Rolando, Grayford Gray, George Spain, Elisabeth Rukeyser, June Palmer, Governor Don Sundquist, Evelyn Robertson, Carol Westlake, Rep. Mary Ann Eckles, Gaylon Booker, Debi Tate and Ben Dishman. June 23, 2000.

the Staff . . .
1962

Most of the personnel of the Wills Center children's division are pictured above in a staff meeting. Acting Director Dr. H. James Crecraft is seated in the center. Others are, left to right, Dr. Charles Corbin, fellow in child psychiatry; Dr. James Gammill, child analyst; Clinton Griffin and William Boyd, teachers at the Wills Center School; Dr. John Pate, director of the School; George Spain, social worker; Mrs. Christine Fossick, teacher; Dr. Margaret Evans, child analyst; Miss Miriam McHaney, chief social worker; Miss Margaret Fernia, professor at the University of Tennessee School of Social Work, a visitor; Mrs. Bransford J. Norton, dietician; Miss Peggy Guess, nursing instructor; Mrs. Randolph Tucker, nursing supervisor; Janice Ricketson, social worker.

1962

1. Merrilee Spain
2. Lana Graves
3. Lorinda Spain
4. Jody Spain
5. Brian Dever
6. Brenda Dever
7. Jennifer Spain
8. Dennis Spain
9. Sherrilan Spain
10. Wendy Spain
11. Sheila Dever
12. Larry Cherry
13. Edith Cherry
14. Agnes Masters
15. Norma Graves
16. Lynch Spain
17. George (Son) Spain
18. George Spain
19. Clevia Spain
20. Arthur Spain
21. Anna Belle Cantrell
22. Buford Spain
23. Virginia Dever
24. Willie Spain
25. Brad Spain
26. Clifton Cherry
27. Agnes' BF
28. Jackie Bowers
29. Pam Bowers
30. Joe Graves
31. Annie Lou Clinard (sister of Clifton)
32. Maude Cherry (mother of Clifton)
33. Morris Dever
34. Alwyna Dever
35. Dottie Spain
36. Brenda Cantrell
37. Wilma Cantrell
38. Sadie Spain
39. Jill Spain
40. George Edward Spain
41. Jackie Spain

Eleven long years have passed since Jackie died. As the time grew longer and longer I became lonely to lean against the side of a woman, to snuggle against, to talk to. And then it happened. One Sunday, at the end of Earl Lavender's class at Church a hand touched my back. I turned and there was a nice looking woman I did not know – Elizabeth Chrisman. As I learned later she was a retired Vanderbilt Psychiatric nurse. She said she would like to talk with me. Maybe it was brought about by my presenting views sometimes different than others. Whatever it was, she's been an answer to my loneliness. We love each other.

Elizabeth Chrisman

I am a part of all that I have met;
Yet all experience is an arch wherethro'
Gleams that untravell'd world where margin fades
For ever and forever when I move.
How dull it is to pause, to make an end,
To rust unburnish'd, not to shine in use!
As tho' to breathe were life! Life piled on life
Were all too little, and of one to me
Little remains: but every hour is saved
From that eternal silence, something more,
A bringer of new things; and vile it were
For some three suns to store and hoard myself,
And this gray spirit yearning in desire
To follow knowledge like a sinking star,
Beyond the utmost bound of human thought.

That ever with a frolic welcome took
The thunder and the sunshine, and opposed
Free hearts, free foreheads-you and I are old;
Old age hath yet his honor and his toil.
Death closes all; but something ere the end,
Some work of noble note, may yet be done,
Not unbecoming men that strove with gods.
The lights begin to twinkle from the rocks;
The long day wanes; the slow moon climbs; the deep
Moans round with many voices. Come my friends,
'Tis not too late to seek a newer world.
Push off, and sitting well in order smile
The rounding furrows; for my purpose holds
To sail beyond the sunset, and the baths
Of all the western stars, until I die.

Though much is taken, much abides; and though
We are not now that strength which in old days
Moved earth and heaven, that which we are, we are,
One equal temper of heroic hearts,
Made weak by time and fate, but strong in will
To strive, to seek, to find, and not to yield.

Alfred Lord Tennyson, *Ulysses*

I guess I'll end here with Gus's words –
"Well my God Woodrow, It's been quite a party."

George Spain

*****

HOLY BIBLE

CLARKE'S
COMMENTARY.

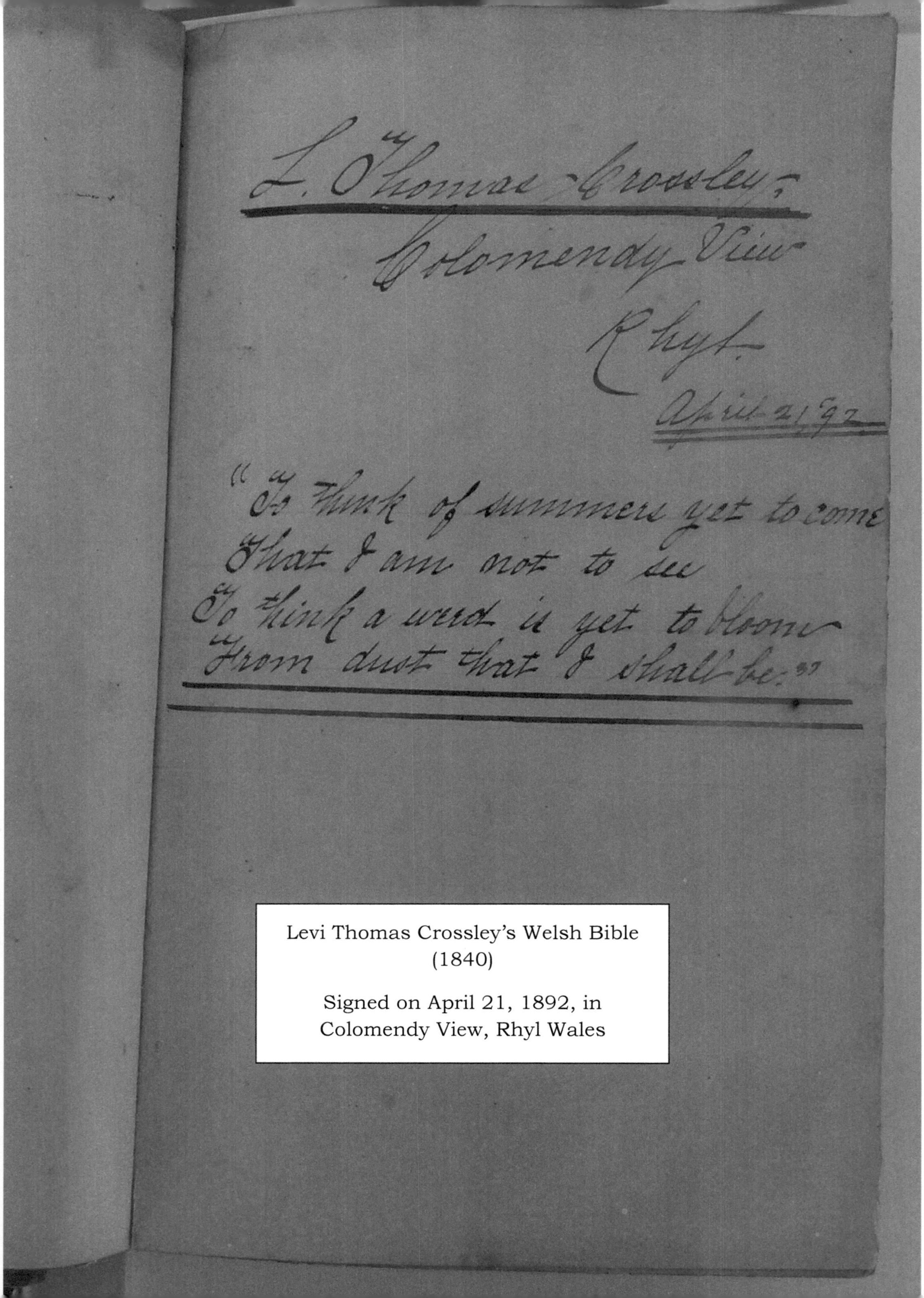

L. Thomas Crossley,

Colomendy View

Rhyl.

April 21, 92

" "To think of summers yet to come
That I am not to see
To think a weed is yet to bloom
From dust that I shall be.""

Levi Thomas Crossley's Welsh Bible
(1840)

Signed on April 21, 1892, in
Colomendy View, Rhyl Wales

YR

ESBONIAD BERNIADOL;

NEU

DDEONGLIADAU LLYTHYRENOL, ATHRAWIAETHOL, AC YMARFEROL,

AR YR

Hen Destament a'r Newydd;

YN CYNWYS

GWAHANOL OLYGIADAU PRIF FERNIAID Y BYD,

AR

DDUWINYDDIAETH, BRUDIAETH, A HANESIAETH YR YSGRYTHYRAU SANTAIDD.

YN CHWANEGOL AT SYLWADAU DIWYGIEDIG

Y PARCH. ADAM CLARKE, LL.D., F.A.S.,

M.R.I.A., &c., &c., &c.,

A NODIADAU DUWINYDDOL Y PARCH. J. BENSON, &c.

"Canys pa bethau bynag a ysgrifenwyd o'r blaen, er addysg i ni yr ysgrifenwyd hwynt: fel trwy amynedd a dyddanwch yr ysgrythyrau, y gallem gael gobaith." RHUF. xv. 4.

WEDI EI OLYGU A'I GYFIEITHU YN OFALUS

GAN JOHN JONES, LLANIDLOES,

(IDRISYN.)

CYFROL IV.

MATTHEW HYD YR ACTAU.

LLANIDLOES:

A GYHOEDDWYD GAN EDWARD JONES,

AC AR WERTH GAN YR HOLL WEINIDOGION WESLEYAIDD, A CHAN Y GWAHANOL LYFRWERTHWYR.

1840.

John Crossley, Father of the following
sons & daughters:—
Grace Crossley, Mother of the aforesaid
sons & daughters:—

Births

1st Thomas Crossley, son of John & Grace
Crossley, born 16th March, 1855, at half past
9 o'clock in the morning.

2nd John Crossley, son of the above named
man & wife, born 15th April, 1856, at 4 o'clock
in the morning.

3rd Jane Crossley, daughter of the aforemen-
tioned couple, born 26th June, 1858, at 4 o'clock
in the evening.

4th Emryo Bonair Crossley, likewise son of the
above-mentioned John & Grace Crossley, born
27th November, 1859, at 3 o'clock in the
morning.

5th Levi Thomas Crossley, son of John &
Grace Crossley, born 27th January, 1863,
at 8 o'clock in the evening.

6th Miriam Crossley, daughter of John & Grace

Crossley, born 28th October, 1864, at 3 o'clock in the Afternoon.

7th Reuben Crossley, Son of the above designated man & wife, born 10th February, 1866, at 10. o'clock in the morning.

8th Price Crossley, also son of the aforesaid Couple, born 9th July, 1868, at 2. o'clock in the afternoon.

9th Harriet Crossley, daughter of John & Grace Crossley born 2nd February, 1870, at 11 o'clock in the morning.

Deaths

Thomas Crossley, eldest son of John & Grace Crossley, died 26th July, 1860; aged 5 Years and 4 Months.

Also Jane Crossley daughter of John & Grace Crossley, died 6th May, 1861, aged 3 Years, 4 Months, & 1 day.

"At rest with Jesus."

In Memory Of Levi Thomas
Crossley, Who Went To Sea, 1881

Thy parents old are yearning
With hearts of grief and pain
Their eyes are dim with watching
To see thee home again.

Their footsteps now are feeble
Their lives are fading fast—
Oh! come once more to see them
Before their lives be past—

Thy brothers, too, are longing
To see thee home once more,
Come, tell us, brother Levi,
Will thou return no more?

We still keep on expecting
That thou'lt return some day,—
God grant, ere long, we find thee
Upon thy homeward way

Thy sisters, too, so loving
Would welcome thee with tears;
But now their hearts are brimming
With anxious cares and fears.

Farewell! farewell we bid thee, —
If thou'lt return no more
Our hope is that thou'rt gone to Heaven,
That holier, happier shore
———"———

We'll each strive there to meet thee,
Then joy, indeed, 'twill be
To sing our Saviour's praises
In company with thee.
———"——— R. Crossley
———"———

The one that now is speaking
Ere long shall be at rest
Beneath some church-yard tomb-stone,
Cold clay shall form the nest;
And friends may come o'er me to weep,
From North, South, East and West;
Yet though my body there be found,
My soul shall be at rest
———"———
Reuben Crossley, to his affec-
tionale Brother,
Levi.
———"———
Please write to
know this

§ 32. Believers His Children.

Is. lxiii. 8. For he said, Surely they are my people, children that will not lie; so he was their Saviour.
Rom. viii. 14. For as many as are led by the Spirit of God, they are the sons of God.
Gal. iii. 26. For ye are all the children of God by faith in Christ Jesus.
— iv. 5. To redeem them that were under the law, that we might receive the adoption of sons.
— — 6. And because ye are sons, God hath sent forth the Spirit of his Son into your hearts, crying, Abba, Father.
Eph. ii. 19. Now therefore ye are no more strangers and foreigners, but fellow citizens with the saints, and of the household of God;
— v. 1. Be ye therefore followers of God, as dear children;
1 Pet. i. 14. As obedient children, not fashioning yourselves according to the former lusts in your ignorance;
1 John iii. 1. Behold, what manner of love the Father hath bestowed upon us, that we should be called the sons of God: therefore the world knoweth us not, because it knew him not.

§ 33. Heirs of God, and Joint Heirs with Christ.

Rom. viii. 16. The Spirit itself beareth witness with our spirit, that we are the children of God:
— — 17. And if children, then heirs; heirs of God, and joint heirs with Christ; if so be that we suffer with him, that we may be also glorified together.
Gal. iv. 7. Wherefore thou art no more a servant, but a son; and if a son, then an heir of God through Christ.
Tit. iii. 7. That being justified by his grace, we should be made heirs according to the hope of eternal life.

§ 34. Chastened.

Heb. xii. 9. Furthermore, we have had fathers of our flesh which corrected us, and we gave them reverence: shall we not much rather be in subjection unto the Father of Spirits, and live?
— — 10. For they verily for a few days chastened us after their own pleasure; but he for our profit, that we might be partakers of his holiness.
Rev. iii. 19. As many as I love, I rebuke and chasten: be zealous therefore, and repent.

CHAP. VIII.

DUTIES AND GRACES OF THE NEW LIFE.

35. Love to God and Man.

1 Cor. xiii. 1. Though I speak with the tongues of men and of angels, and have not charity, I am become as sounding brass, or a tinkling cymbal.
— — 2. And though I have the gift of prophecy, and understand all mysteries, and all knowledge; and though I have all faith, so that I could remove mountains, and have not charity, I am nothing.
— — 3. And though I bestow all my goods to feed the poor, and though I give my body to be burned, and have not charity, it profiteth me nothing.
— — 4. Charity suffereth long, and is kind; charity envieth not; charity vaunteth not itself, is not puffed up,
— — 5. Doth not behave itself unseemly, seeketh not her own, is not easily provoked, thinketh no evil;
— — 6. Rejoiceth not in iniquity, but rejoiceth in the truth;
— — 7. Beareth all things, believeth all things, hopeth all things, endureth all things.
— — 8. Charity never faileth: but whether there be prophecies, they shall fail; whether there be tongues, they shall cease; whether there be knowledge, it shall vanish away.

— — 9. For we know in part, and we prophesy in part.
— — 10. But when that which is perfect is come, then that which is in part shall be done away.
— — 11. When I was a child, I spake as a child, I understood as a child, I thought as a child: but when I became a man, I put away childish things.
— — 13. And now abideth faith, hope, charity, these three; but the greatest of these is charity.
— xiv. 1. Follow after charity, and desire spiritual gifts, but rather that ye may prophesy.
2 John 6. And this is love, that we walk after his commandments. This is the commandment, That, as ye have heard from the beginning, ye should walk in it.

(A. THE MEASURE OF LOVE.)

Luke vii. 40. And Jesus answering said unto him, Simon, I have somewhat to say unto thee. And he saith, Master, say on.
— — 41. There was a certain creditor which had two debtors: the one owed five hundred pence, and the other fifty.
— — 42. And when they had nothing to pay, he frankly forgave them both. Tell me therefore, which of them will love him most?
— — 43. Simon answered and said, I suppose that he, to whom he forgave most. And he said unto him, Thou hast rightly judged.

§ 36. Love to Man.

Mat. vii. 12. Therefore all things whatsoever ye would that men should do to you, do ye even so to them: for this is the law and the prophets.
— xix. 18. He saith unto him, Which? Jesus said, Thou shalt do no murder, Thou shalt not commit adultery, Thou shalt not steal, Thou shalt not bear false witness,
— — 19. Honour thy father and thy mother: and, Thou shalt love thy neighbour as thyself.
— xxii. 39. And the second is like unto it, Thou shalt love thy neighbour as thyself.
— — 40. On these two commandments hang all the law and the prophets.
Mark xii. 31. And the second is like, namely this, Thou shalt love thy neighbour as thyself. There is none other commandment greater than these.
Luke vi. 31. And as ye would that men should do to you, do ye also to them likewise.
Rom. xiii. 8. Owe no man anything, but to love one another: for he that loveth another hath fulfilled the law.
— — 9. For this, Thou shalt not commit adultery, Thou shalt not kill, Thou shalt not steal, Thou shalt not bear false witness, Thou shalt not covet; and if there be any other commandment, it is briefly comprehended in this saying, namely, Thou shalt love thy neighbour as thyself.
— — 10. Love worketh no ill to his neighbour: therefore love is the fulfilling of the law.
Gal. v. 14. For all the law is fulfilled in one word, even in this; Thou shalt love thy neighbour as thyself.
Jam. ii. 8. If ye fulfil the royal law according to the Scripture, Thou shalt love thy neighbour as thyself, ye do well:

§ 37. Love to Christian Brethren.

John xiii. 34. A new commandment I give unto you, That ye love one another; as I have loved you, that ye also love one another.
— — 35. By this shall all men know that ye are my disciples, if ye have love one to another.
— xv. 12. This is my commandment, That ye love one another, as I have loved you.
— — 17. These things I command you, that ye love one another.
Rom. xii. 9. Let love be without dissimulation. Abhor that which is evil; cleave to that which is good.
— — 10. Be kindly affectioned one to another with brotherly love; in honour preferring one another;
1 Cor. xvi. 14. Let all your things be done with charity.

Col. iii. 14. And above all these things *put on* charity, which is the bond of perfectness.
1 Thess. iv. 9. But as touching brotherly love ye need not that I write unto you; for ye yourselves are taught ...

... commandment is ... good conscience,

...

... our souls in ... ... with love of a pure ...

... vent char ... ... er the multi-

... w command-... meet unto you, but ... ... ment which ye had from the beginning ... commandment is the word which ye have heard from the beginning.

— 10. He that loveth his brother abideth in the light, and there is none occasion of stumbling in him.
— iii. 10. In this the children of God are manifest, and the children of the devil; whosoever doeth not righteousness is not of God, neither he that loveth not his brother.

— 11. For this is the message that ye heard from the beginning, that we should love one another.
— 14. We know that we have passed from death unto life, because we love the brethren. He that loveth not *his* brother abideth in death.
— 18. My little children, let us not love in word, neither in tongue; but in deed and in truth.
— iv. 7. Beloved, let us love one another: for love is of God; and every one that loveth is born of God, and knoweth God.
— 11. Beloved, if God so loved us, we ought also to love one another.
2 John 5. And now I beseech thee, lady, not as though I wrote a new commandment unto thee, but that which we had from the beginning, that we love one another.

(A. THE NECESSARY CONSEQUENCE OF LOVING ...

1 John v. 2. By this we know that we love the ... dren of God, when we love God, and keep his com... mandments.
— iv. 20. If a man say ... brother, he is a liar ...

...

Rom. xvi. 17. N... them which cause d... the doctrine which ye h... — 18. For they ... such serve not our Lord Jesus Christ, but their own belly; and by good words and fair speeches deceive the hearts of the simple.
1 Cor. i. 10. Now I beseech you, brethren, by the name of our Lord Jesus Christ, that ye all speak the same thing, and *that* there be no divisions among you; but *that* ye be perfectly joined together in the same mind and in the same judgment.
— 11. For it hath been declared unto me of you, my brethren, by them *which are of the house* of Chloe, that there are contentions among you.
— 12. Now this I say, that every one of you ... I am of Paul; and I of Apollos; and I of Ce... and I of Christ.
— 13. Is Christ divided? was Paul crucified for ... were ye baptized in the name of Paul?
— And I, brethren, could not speak unto you ... spiritual, but as unto carnal, *even* as unto babes ...

... have fed you with milk, and not with ... ye were not able to *bear it,* neither ... ... ye are yet carnal: for whereas *there is* ...

among you envying, and strife, and divisions, are ye not carnal, and walk as men?
— 4. For while one saith, I am of Paul; and another, I *am* of Apollos; are ye not carnal?
— 5. Who then is Paul, and who *is* Apollos, but ministers by whom ye believed, even as the Lord gave to every man?

(2. BY GOING TO LAW BEFORE THE HEATHEN.)

1 Cor. vi. 1. Dare any of you, having a matter against another, go to law before the unjust, and not before the saints?
— 2. Do ye not know that the saints shall judge the world? and if the world shall be judged by you, are ye unworthy to judge the smallest matters?
— 3. Know ye not that we shall judge angels? how much more things that pertain to this life?
— 4. If then ye have judgments of things pertaining to this life, set them to judge who are least esteemed in the church.
— 5. I speak to your shame. Is it so, that there is not a wise man among you? no, not one that shall be able to judge between his brethren?
— 6. But brother goeth to law with brother, and that before the unbelievers.
— 7. Now therefore there is utterly a fault among you, because ye go to law one with another. Why do ye not rather take wrong? Why do you not rather *suffer yourselves to be defrauded?*

§ 39. *Christian Unity.*

... 5. Now the ... patience and consola-... be like ... one toward another ... ... Jesus ... ... ye may ... mind *and* one mouth glorify God, even the Fa... our Lord Jesus Christ.
— 7. Wherefore recei... e one another, as Christ also received us, to the glo... f God.
Phil. ii. 1. If *there* be th... re any consolation in Christ, if any comfort of lov... any fellowship of the Spirit, if any ... ls and me... ... ... at ye be likeminded, ... accord, of one mind.
... beseech Syntyche, ... e Lord.
... e mind, having ... brethren, be

... led Didy... ... that we

... een much ... e in these ... y years to ... ... urney ... o Spain, ... st to ... you i... ny jour-... you, ... , and ... into ... ... unto ... the ... now ... s of ... the house of ... ... to the Achaia, and *that* ... ... ministry of the sa... ... ch, and
— 16. That ... ... th.
— 17. I am g... ... ing of St... nas and to every one that h... ... lacking Fortunatus and Ac... ... of that which on your part they have supplied.
— 18. For they have refreshed my spirit and yours: therefore acknowledge ye them that are such.
2 Cor. i. 23. Moreover I call God for a record upon my soul, that to spare you I came not as yet unto Corinth.

TCHCOCK'S

NEW AND

PLETE ANALYSIS

OF THE

OLY BIBLE

The Holy Bible

JOHNSON & SON

George Spain is a native of Nashville, Tennessee. He worked for fifty-two years in mental health as a therapist and CEO of Centerstone, Inc. He has authored fifteen books: *Our People: Stories of the South, Lost Cove, Come Sit With Me, Delightful Suthun Madnesses XIII, The Last Giant, Our People: More Stories of the South, JoJo's Christmas, Sundancing With Crazy Horse, Jackie, They Are Us: What People With Mental Illness Have Taught Me, The Official One and Only Imperial Wizard Approved KKK Hall of Fame Guide Book* (a satire), *Deep in Darkness, Dreaming the Fire Away, The Cherokee Five & The Cussin' Tree* and *My Creators.*